# America's War On Syria : Donald Trump 's Attack on Biochemical Weapons : Myth or Truth?

By reading this document, the reader agrees that under no circumstances are is the author responsible for any losses, direct or indirect, which are incurred as a result of the use of information contained within this document, including, but not limited to, —errors, omissions, or inaccuracies.

# You might Also Be Interested In..

LINK: *https://amzn.to/2LqHaCU*

# Chapter 1:  US Pretentious and Selfish Intervention in Syria

In September 2016, the Western media reported that the Syrian government of Bashar al Assad had used deadly chemical weapons on its own civilians. Similar allegations had been made back in August 2013, and President Obama, addressing the media, had said it was believed Assad had on several occasions that year attacked his own people with chemical weapons. Besides, in July 2012, the Syrian government, through its Ministry of Foreign Affairs, had admitted having stockpiles of chemical weapons.

The question is: Has the US or any other Western nation ever attacked Syria on account of the regime's alleged ill treatment of its people prior to 2018? The reality is that they have condemned such atrocities but they have not been proactive in stopping them.

Yet in early April 2018 when the Western media reported that the government of Bashar al Assad had used deadly chemical weapons on civilians, the US went full throttle putting plans in place to make an immediate attack on Syria. The alleged chemical attack took place on April 7, and the US in league with its allies, Britain and France, launched missiles on Syria just a week later, on April 14. In addition, they threatened that they would attack Syria again if the regime dared to use chemical weapons again.

As the Western allies' Joint Chief of Staff's chairman was busy explaining the strategic locations their missiles had hit in Syria, Vladimir Putin, the Russian President, made a point of letting the West know he did not like it that they had attacked Syria. The chairman, General Joseph Dunford Jr, clarified that the allied forces had struck a scientific research centre very close to Syria's capital, Damascus, a facility close to Syria's city of Homs thought to be a chemical weapons' storage, as well as a command post, also close to Homs; a total of three key locations.

Whereas the report of the action by the Western allies as crafted sounded morally right and justifiable, one cannot fail to wonder what in this case of alleged Syrian chemical attack was different from past attacks the regime has been accused of perpetrating. A lot of what people believe about Syria is what the Western media has told them, yet it is true it has been accused of bias in the past, including in the reporting of the 2016 US presidential election when President Donald Trump won. Media critics have said it gave President Trump an unfair advantage over Hillary Clinton by covering his crowd pulling rallies without pay, making the competition skewed towards him as a candidate. In short, critics reckon the Western media is not to be blindly trusted.

By the same token, one wonders if the Western media is also not biased in its reporting about Syria and the internal war that has been going on to-date. The US has been known to enjoy playing the Big Brother role at the world stage, but some sober minded Americans have over the years been questioning their country's tactics in exerting its presence. For instance, after the second Gulf War, a number of countries began to criticize America openly, and while the citizenry was proud of the efforts shown by their soldiers, a good part became critical of the war especially when it became clear Iraq did not have stocks of weapons of mass destruction (WMD).

It is a fact the US has on some occasions bulldozed its way around the world, influencing how governments are run in other countries, but every time there is some implicit US interest in the agenda. Yet on that count, the American populace does not seem concerned. However, no US president, other than Trump, has picked a fight with major global organizations, including those that attempt to inject sobriety into global decision making. He has often criticized the role of the UN and other global organizations that endeavor to ensure there is fairness in decisions made regarding the sovereignty of nations and general global welfare. However, this is not surprising as he still criticized those international bodies during his presidential campaign, citing the hefty expenses the US was incurring in supporting those organizations.

## *The US Has Fought Some Countries and Ignored Others for Selfish Reasons*

In December 2016, Trump criticized the United Nations (UN) after the passing of a resolution demanding that Israel stops increasing its Gaza settlements. Of course, President Trump, like many Americans, would like to see Israel subdue the Palestinians to make it easier for the US to access the oil resources in the region. In the meantime, Americans are not perturbed by the decision of the Trump's administration to attack Syria. To them, a weakened Syria is an advantage to its external enemies.

Before this April intervention by the US and its allies, America found it alright for Syria to wear itself down as long as it was through an internal war, because the situation of a Syria weakened militarily and financially was good particularly for America and Israel. The raging civil war in Syria has been weakening the country without its enemies, US and Israel, having to spend a cent. In other wars where Syria has been involved, the US has had to spend its taxpayers' money to influence the outcome of the war by supporting Syria's enemies either financially, materially, or both.

And even without any wars going on, the US has given support to Israel to build its military capacity whenever the two countries deemed it necessary, from way back in the 1960s. With a tamed Syria and stability in the Gulf region, America's supply of oil is not threatened, and its economy is, therefore, not at jeopardy.

In 1990 when the US fought to push Iraqi forces out of Kuwait, not only liberating Kuwait but taking the fight right into Iraqi territory, the greatest motivation had been the resources the US stood to gain from the Middle East. With the US involvement in the region,

Americans are able to ensure they access oil at reasonable prices, and American companies enjoy a good share of oil-related contracts. And after every war, there are always beneficiaries of reconstruction contracts, and in the case of the Middle East, the US is among the leading ones.

The family of former presidents Bush, for example, through the Carlyle Group and other firms, became a great beneficiary of the Gulf War. In 2001, the president who led the 1990/91 Gulf War, George Herbert Walker Bush, or Bush Senior, was reported to have traveled to the Middle East as an ambassador for the Carlyle Group, which is a multi-billion dollar company with much of its shareholding in the hands of American ex-government officials. This is essentially a war benefit by Americans, and it gains a somewhat sinister look when linked to a former president.

Other government officials like former Vice-President, Dick Cheney, had their slices of the Middle-East pie as well. When he left office and was contemplating running for president, Cheney raised substantial amounts of money in preparation for his eventual campaign, and what is amazing is that many of his donors ended up winning big contracts in Iraq, the country he and Bush senior had led in fighting. Names like Thomas Cruikshank of Halliburton, Stephen Bechtel, the billionaire of Bechtel Corporation, and Duane Andrews, of Science Applications International Corporation (SAIC), all have surfaced in the Federal Election Commission (FEC) as good examples of war beneficiaries who had links with the former VP.

Their conglomerates had ties with the former US Vice-president and his colleague, Secretary of State in the Bush administration, Donald Rumsfeld, and they ended up earning big monies from the fallen Iraq. Such eventualities often raise eyebrows and leave America exposed about its self interest in attacking other countries or influencing their leadership.

With such examples of US self-interest as that in the Iraqi War, one can reasonably question the motive behind attacks on other countries like Syria. When former President George W. Bush took over office as President of the US, America's selfish interest began to manifest in an even bigger way, enticing it into an opportune war. In fact, Bush began another war with Iraq and although some Americans were apprehensive about the second Gulf War, the administration went ahead to lead some other Western countries such as Britain in attacking Iraq.

In the first Gulf War, Bush Senior had the support of many more countries, including Arab countries, than his son had in the second Gulf War. It was understandable that countries like Syria would give support in that first war at the time considering the sovereignty of Kuwait, a fellow Arab country, was at stake. However, in the second instance, US self-interest was too glaring to ignore, and Syria did not participate. That stance which Syria took cannot have gone down well with the US, and must have put it in the Big Brother's bad books. Yet even France that had contributed 17,000 troops in the liberation of Kuwait was against that second attack on Iraq in 2003.

Donald Trump, who was a prominent businessman at the time, was pro-war as George W. Bush threatened to attack Iraq, then he began to waver and being non-committal as the war raged on and as the tide seemed to blow against the US. In fact, it was only a year and a half later when it became clear to the world the war was unwarranted that he began to express opposition to it. From a business perspective, he did not find anything wrong with the war, and like other pro-war

Americans, he saw an America that was asserting itself in the Middle East for the benefit of the country. After all, the ill feelings against the perpetrators of the 9/11 bomb attacks were still strong, and any country thought to have provided a safe haven for terrorists was frowned upon by the West.

In the second Gulf War, the list of countries the US flaunted as being in support of the war was not convincing of genuine support for the war. Many of the said countries were either beneficiaries of basic support from the US, while others were trying to suck up to the Big Brother to earn future support of one kind or another. Others like Ethiopia and Eritrea who had an on and off border conflict between them just wanted to be in good books with the US in case the nemesis went rogue in the future, in which case the US might come in handy in offering protection. Among the countries that made the list of US supporters in the war were Albania, Bulgaria, Croatia, Estonia, Latvia, Lithuania, Macedonia, Romania, Slovakia and Slovenia, which either aspired to join NATO or had their case to join NATO pending. And the US, obviously, had a lot of influence within NATO.

Other countries like Egypt, Israel, the Czech Republic, Hungary, Turkey and a few others, provided air bases, over-flight permission and little else, while others simply offered the US moral support but refused outright to join in the war that they thought was either unjustifiable or premature. Of course, Kuwait had little choice in the position it was going to take, considering the US had engaged in the first Gulf War to liberate it. Besides, Kuwait is always glad to know the US has its back in case of provocation, not only by Iraq, but also by Iran or Saudi Arabia.

What is curious is that the Bush presidents who led both Gulf Wars are said to have had business links with family members of people from the region deemed to be of dubious character; Osama bin Laden being a case in point. The same Carlyle Group mentioned earlier was reported by the Wall Street Journal (WSJ) in 2001 as having had ties with companies in Saudi Arabia in which the bin Laden family had invested. In short, besides the country entering into war for its own interest, individual Americans seemed to have vested interests as well.

Even for people with no interest in Syria, there have been worse cases in the past where they wished someone would have intervened to bring sanity into the country, especially when pictures of children victims of alleged chemical weapons were flashed on TV screens across the world. Yet, like in 2016, the US stood aloof. After trying in vain to weaken Iran through sanctions, the US decided to court it; a nemesis who also happens to be Syria's ally. In 2015, together with other UN members, the US entered into an arms deal with Iran. At the moment, therefore, Iran does not seem a likely threat to America, and as such there has not been any immediate need for the US to save Syria either as a regime or as a community. If Iran had appeared to be a threat, the US might have wanted to help Syria stabilize so it could be its pawn in one way or another in fighting Iran.

If Iran were to fight Iraq or any of the oil producing countries in the region, the aftermath would be expensive for the US and other Western countries that have always relied on the region's oil to grow their economies.

On this count, Syria has no oil resources that would interest America and is hence of little consequence to the US as a country. In short, Syria has not been of much use to the US in the recent past, either politically or economically, and as long as it is not affecting stability in the oil producing region, the US does not care much what goes on internally. From America's conduct over the years, it is apparent its foreign policy has an implicit provision that seeks to establish what-is-in-it-for-the US before getting involved with another country.

When it comes to Iran and Syria, their relationship with the US at any one time has been one of convenience. The US does not particularly like either of them. It is not at all like the relationship the US has had with Israel. For instance, during the Iran-Iraq war of the 1980s when Iraq invaded Iran and the war raged on for years, Syria had sided with Iran, and the US had backed Iraq. Obviously, Iraq and the US must have identified a common enemy this time, albeit by proxy. They have now been watching Syria destroy its people and its resources, and that is to the advantage of the US if only no significant terror threats crop up in the process.

Making the relationship between the US and Syria more unfriendly was the fact that by backing Iran, Syria had antagonized many Arab countries, and some like Saudi Arabia are key US allies. In fact, Saudi Arabia has been calling for the removal of Bashar-al-Assad's regime from power, and it has even severed diplomatic ties with Syria. In 2012, Saudi Arabia closed its Damascus embassy and expelled the Syrian ambassador from Saudi Arabia. In short, neither the US nor its allies, Saudi Arabia and Israel have any genuine sympathies for Syria. If they ever back the country, it is for selfish reasons.

The US is particularly keen on its interests considering the erratic way in which it has behaved towards other countries. The infamous Gulf Wars were waged against a regime that the same US had armed earlier, still for its own gains. It was Saddam Hussein's regime that invaded Iran in the early 1980's, and instead of considering that the sovereignty of Iran had been violated, the US, a country that preaches democracy and respect for everyone, backed the invading party. The Reagan administration even sold helicopters and aircrafts to Iraq as the war went on, purporting to make the sales of the machinery for civilian use. In addition, the US gave food aid to Iraq and shared crucial battlefield intelligence with them.

So, even without sending its own foot soldiers to help Iraq, the US did help improve the fighting conditions for the Iraqis at the expense of the Iranians. Obviously, the US aid left Iraq with spare money to use on buying armaments and to pay for war logistics. The US all along wanted an opportunity to exploit Iraq for its oil resources, and in this instance, it helped strengthen its petrodollar. There were also many American corporations that were contracted to render services in Iraq during and after the war. So, despite the unnecessary loss of lives that took place and the massive debt the US accumulated when the war took longer than anticipated, there were still Americans who made a kill from the war.

As for George W. Bush, he wanted to give a different face to America after the earlier showdown between Bush Senior and the Iraq regime. He wanted to ensure Saddam Hussein was toppled. The US was particularly obsessed with the crush of Saddam Hussein's regime to satisfy the wish of its ally, Israel, which saw Iraq as a real threat to its existence. Iraq has always been a staunch supporter of the Palestinian Arabs, even in the olden days when they were still under the Palestinian Liberation Organization (PLO) led by Yasser Arafat. Even as the Gulf War raged on, the two parties were still great allies.

Such closeness made both of them enemies of the US and Israel, and it was easy for the US to enter into a proxy war under any pretext. After all, many US congressmen enjoy great financial support from rich Israelis during their campaigns, and it then becomes easy for such financiers to influence decision making in the US. The US beneficiaries, on their part, feel obliged to do the bidding of the state of Israel, including some questionable wars such as the one the US entered into under the pretext Iraq had accumulated weapons of mass destruction (WMD) and was unduly oppressing its citizens. In this case, US' wish to help install a regime that would help America have better access to Iraq's oil led the administration to engage in a war under the guise of pre-emptying terrorist activity and liberating the people of Iraq from a dictator.

A similar attack occurred in Libya when President Muammar Gaddafi, who for years resisted any attempts to establish ties with the US, refused to do the bidding of America. When he took power in 1969, Gaddafi forced the US companies in the country to vacate, and he went ahead to nationalize those oil companies. Obviously, by Gaddafi bringing US oil businesses in Libya to an end must have hurt the US financially to some degree, a move that was also humiliating to a world power. It was with that venom that the US took part in the overthrow of Gaddafi in 2011, by rendering support to the rebels in form of air strikes that were aimed at the Libyan army. Overtly, of course, the US purported to liberate the Libyan people from a dictator and to bring democracy to the Arab country.

In short, the US does not rush to render support to any country on moral grounds or as an obligation of a powerful country. Instead, it seeks to protect its interests or to find an avenue to exploit the other country's resources. If that were not the case, America would have rushed to try and bring sanity to Cambodia during dictator Pol Pot's regime in the 1970s or to the East African country of Luanda during the genocide of 1994. Neither of those countries has oil or any significant natural resource that would interest the US.

In the case of Syria, it is in US' interest to have the regime and the country as a whole weakened, because it leaves the country with internal problems to deal with and little resources to spare in supporting regimes like Iran that are a pain to the US and its friend, Israel. In supporting Assad in the fight against rebels, Iran has spent a lot of money and lost soldiers, including senior ones in the rank of general. To the US, this is a plus, as Iran is likely to be left weaker, both financially and in terms of military power, and in that situation it is unlikely to threaten any of the oil producing Arab countries the US benefits from.

**The Real Reasons the US Attacked Assad's Regime**


One reason the Trump administration decided to attack Syria was to give the president a break from the depressing domestic situation. Critics of President Trump have been having a field day at home, with the Mueller investigation going on. With his former aides such as Michael Flynn and Rick Gates having accepted to testify in the investigation that is looking into Russia's involvement in the latest US presidential elections, and with the possibility of them entering into a plea bargain agreement, the president needed a distraction to get the media attention on something else other than the possibility of his impeachment.

To make matters worse, besides the Russia involvement there was the scandalous alleged sexual affair involving Stormy Daniels, a former adult film actress, and Donald Trump, and both led to the raid on the office of Trump's lawyer, which became headline news.

For a president who has already been scandalized by the reflection of a chaotic White House, and one who has been portrayed as being minimally knowledgeable by author Michael Wolff in his book, Fire and Fury that was released in January 2018, the latter scandals could be the straw that broke the camel's back and President Trump knows it. Hence, one reason for the attack on Syria was to serve as a means to divert the attention of the American populace from the debate as to whether their president warranted impeachment or not.

Then there is the issue of Russia's interference with the Syrian civil war, where Russia has been asserting its presence and making itself visible to the world as a powerhouse. Conversely, the US wanted to enter Syria to pass a message to Russia that it is not the only global powerhouse, and that the US could influence matters in the region at will as well.

The US was not happy that Russia was going to determine the way forward for Syria after the dust is settled, which is inevitable if Russia is the only big foreign power purporting to remedy the situation. It also must have unsettled the US to have Syria seek to become a close ally of Russia at the expense of the US, because for the sake of oil resources in the Middle East and the safety of Israel, the US would like as many Arab allies as possible. In short, one important motivation for the US' involvement in the Syrian war was to make its power and influence felt by Russia; a proxy war.

Of course, when Russia first joined the war in September 2015, it was on Syria's request for military assistance as al Assad's regime tried to subdue the attacking rebels and the emboldened jihadist groups. Before the overt military airstrikes in the rebel dominated regions of Syria, Russia had concentrated on supplying armaments to the Syrian army. In the past, the US has influenced resolutions by the UN Security Council and led military forces in keeping countries across the world secure, and this has served to keep Russia from being a military bully anywhere in the world. US' real and perceived military power has also kept China from trying to exert its military might the way it has been doing with its economic might.

In fact, China has in the recent past tried to assess US reaction when it laid a claim to the

South China Sea. If Russia got away with influencing the outcome of the Syrian war and the rebuilding of the country, the US' presumed global power would be put to question. As such, countries like Russia and China might feel more confident interfering with other sovereign countries, either annexing them or exploiting their resources.

It is also clear that Syria values the assistance it has been receiving from Iran, a country that has for long been at loggerheads with the US, mainly for its stance on the issue of accumulation of nuclear arms. Revamping its good relations with Syria, with Russia as their ally, leaves US sidelined and looking weak in influence, yet the US has always cherished the position of powerful overseer in matters of sovereignty. Of worry to the US too is the number of regional leaders who have paid courtesy calls on the Russian President since Russia began military action in Syria. Also, as the approval rating of President Trump continues to drop, Putin's domestic approval has been on the rise.

For the US, staying away as atrocities were carried out by both rebels and Assad's regime was like watching a country self-destruct, and leaving Syria weaker militarily and financially would see one more US and Israel nemesis down, and the US influence in the region better placed. Unfortunately, Russia's intervention has put the US in a disadvantaged position as Russia earns the respect of regional leaders and is admired for its military prowess. In the meantime, the US looked lame, weak and inconsequential in a situation that the whole world watched and deemed sensitive. Trump wanted to correct that image of a weak America, and he got that opportunity when Assad allegedly used chemical weapons on Syrian on April 7, 2018.

## Chapter 2: Twisted Truth and Disturbing Past Paradox

Sometimes the US government has supported other sovereign governments in situations that have made the world uncomfortable, owing to such governments' mistreatment of its own citizens. In other instances, it has given outright support to rebels who have not only destabilized governments legitimately in place, but also perpetrated terrorist acts within their own countries.

In the 1970s, for example, the US citizenry, through Congress, had occasion to question the government's involvement in Latin America, when the US helped various governments to train their police forces and even equipped them, only for the world to learn of atrocities allegedly perpetrated by those same forces. In fact, in 1974 specifically, evidence was found that showed there were US trained personnel in Latin America who carried out torture and murder and had multiple disappearances linked to them. Consequently, Congress banned further training of the US to foreign police, and even stopped its supply of equipment to them.

### *The US Used Terrorists to Support Nicaraguan Dictator, Somoza Debayl*

The Nicaraguan situation is a case in point. The Somoza family had led the country since 1936 as a dynasty, and in the second reign of Anastasio Somoza Debayl there was a lot of tension in the country. The reason was not only the continued domination of the Somoza family that continued to get richer by the day at the expense of the general population, but also the dictatorship of Anastasio Somoza. Although his reign saw marked improvement in the economy through modernization of agriculture and industries, and there was significant improvement in the education and health sectors, his second term was rather unsettling.

He ensured the constitution was amended to restrict the number of active political parties in the country, and for most of his second term he put Nicaragua under martial law. Essentially, therefore, his regime had room to violate people's civil rights at will. In this regard, he cracked down on the opposition with an iron fist, particularly the Sardinistas or members of the Sandinista National Liberation Front (FLSN), who had support from the Fidel Castro's Cuban government. In turn, the US gave him support because America was an arch-enemy of Cuba for its communist leanings.

Anastasio Somoza was a product of the US elite academy of cadets, *West Point*, so as a person he knew how to get his way with US officials and could easily appeal for assistance. On the other hand, the US was ready to back anyone at loggerheads with communist and socialist countries, not only because those countries were a threat to the US capitalist system, but also because there was an ongoing campaign between the two ideological blocks to win as many allies as possible. In this regard, the US would not have liked to see the Soviet Union and China win more allies and give the world the impression they were the more powerful block. It is no wonder, therefore, that the US chose to support Nicaragua under Anastasio Somoza.

Before the breakup of the Soviet Union, there was generally only one demarcation in the world political and economic arena, the Soviet Union and its allies and the US and its allies. The rest of the countries, generally termed the non-allied countries, were continually being covertly courted by either side. The two distinct alliances were so sensitive that anyone interfering with a small aligned country was, by implication, attacking its strong ally.

In the case of Nicaragua, the fact that Cuba, which was supporting the contra rebels, had a Communist regime was enough reason for the US to help repel it, even as it helped suppress the efforts by the rebels. It was on that premise that Somoza got the backing of the US despite his high handedness in ruling his country. Still, it is paradoxical how a country such as the US that prides itself with advancing and protecting democracy could support the regime of a leader with dictatorial tendencies.

As usual, the US has always put its interest first. Much as it condemns terrorism, it had no qualms supporting Orlando Bosch Ávila, a Cuban who was a known terrorist, just because he had fallen out with the government of President Fidel Castro. Orlando Bosch became the leader of the Coordination of United Revolutionary Organizations (CURO), a group of rebel organizations that perpetrated terrorist activities against the Cuban government, and which received plenty of support from the CIA of the US.

Another individual, Luis Clemente Faustino Posada Carriles, exemplifies US' paradoxical stance on terrorism and respect for the sovereignty of nations. Carriles, like Bosch, was a Cuban who had fallen out with Fidel Castro's government and escaped into exile. He was also a key member of CURO, and although the FBI identified him as a terrorist, just as Cuba did, the CIA proceeded to recruit him as an agent. Cuba was later to suffer a catastrophe in form of a downed plane, and the Cuban exile turned CIA agent was associated with the bombing of the plane, Flight 455, which caused 73 fatalities.

One would expect the US to consider terrorism a grave crime irrespective of whom the perpetrator or the target is, but it is apparent that is not how America works. As has been seen in the Syrian case, when the crimes target a country of least benefit to the US, it is sufficient for the US to offer public verbal condemnation and nothing tangible. And when it comes to countries like Cuba that has for long been considered an outright enemy of the US, America puts other principles aside and helps to crush the enemy's power and influence. Yet when it comes to a semblance of threat towards the stability of a country that the US hopes to benefit from, a pre-emptive measure like the one that befell Iraq seems warranted.

In the days of the Cold War, the spread of one's ideology was a big deal, and America did whatever it took to get as many countries as possible to adopt its capitalist democratic system, as opposed to the Communist and totalitarian system that dominated the USSR. That position has not exactly changed in the post-cold war days. The only things that seem to have changed are the tactics. Whereas the CIA might hesitate to recruit a known terrorist as its agent, the US does not hesitate to impose economic sanctions on regimes that appear to be a threat to its economic or political success. It is also prepared to go to war on any grounds as long as the end result is expected to safeguard its interest.

In fact, as from 1979 when Syria backed US long-time nemesis, Iran, in the Iran-Iraq War, the US has imposed economic sanctions on the country. It has only eased some of them at its own convenience, mostly those related to US exports. Such sanctions have been imposed on Cuba since 1961, after the country's fight for independence led to its freedom from US domination both economically and politically.

Before then, Cuba had been a US protectorate, following the Treaty of Paris.

There has also been an allegation that the dreaded Taliban was a creation of the US, and that many adherents of Osama bin Laden had been trained by the US. When the US decided to enter into war against the Taliban of Afghanistan, one professor from the University of Georgia, Jeffrey Sommers, claimed, the US had turned against its former benefactors. However, this allegation has been opposed by analysts, including one with The Washington Institute, Michael Rubin.

### *The US Funded and Armed the Mujahedeen against Sovereign Afghanistan; thus the Taliban was Born*

Still, it is a reality that the Taliban was born when the US got into an indirect confrontation with the Soviet Union after the fall of the Afghan monarchy. The Afghan leader in 1973, Zahir Shah, had gone to Italy for eye treatment, and Mohammad Sardar Daoud Khan, who was then Afghanistan's Prime Minister, took over power in a peaceful coup, and he declared the country a republic. Besides the corruption and other unfair tendencies attributed to the royal family, there had been a drought that harmed the economic environment in the country from

1971 to 1972. Consequently, Afghanistan welcomed assistance from the Soviet Union when the strong communist country offered it.

Since the Soviet Union, in its promise to help rebuild the Afghan economy, had not only brought machinery into Afghanistan but its soldiers as well, the US saw a threat in the move. It read a covert strategy by the Soviet Union to spread its ideology and influence in the region. To curb such influence within Central Asia, the US sponsored a disgruntled group, the Mujahedeen, to try and drive out the Soviets. Incidentally, Pakistan and Saudi Arabia accepted to assist the US to enhance the efforts of the Mujahedeen. In fact, much of the recruitment of Mujahedeen fighters was done by the US through ISI, Pakistan's Inter-Services Intelligence.

As much as the US dreads extremism, in this instance, the regime of President Reagan did not mind the Pakistanis using extreme Islamic views to lure the Mujahedeen, who embraced militant means of achieving their goals. Unfortunately, although the US involvement in Afghanistan helped to eject the Soviet Union out of the country, there was a lot of infighting among the Mujahedeen, and ultimately, the

Taliban Movement was born, fully radicalized and militant.

It is a paradox how the US, a country that is known for its advocacy for individual rights would fund and equip a group of Islamic guerrillas to undermine the government of Mohammed Daoud Khan, a president who was committed to reinstating the rights of women, including the right to education and the right to vote. In fact, Khan was bent on eliminating Islamic fundamentalism, a move that would ordinarily have been hailed by the US. However, the fact that he had welcomed the Soviet Union and was working close to the regime which had a divergent ideology and one whose power was a threat to the US, made him unlikeable by the US.

As usual, US economic and political interests come first, and the rest of lost benefits are inevitable opportunity costs. For the many lives that were lost in terrorist activities by the Mujahedeen backed by the US, they were, apparently, unavoidable collateral damage. Still, this now common war by proxy does not leave the big powers entirely unaffected. In the case of the Soviet Union, the prolonged war with the Mujahedeen, which comprised different insurgent groups in Afghanistan, left the communist super power drained of billions of dollars, and the post war effects, including the economic isolation engineered by the US, led to the breakup of the Soviet Union. That happened despite the fact that the Soviet Union had appeared economically and politically stronger than ever after the war.

One thing that put Iran into bad books with the US was that when Ayatollah Ruhollah Khomeini led a revolution against the age old Persian monarchy in Iran, the West lost its influence in the country. Mohammad Reza Shah Pahlavi, who was overthrown in the 1979 Islamic Revolution, had been a friend of the US, and, of course, the US had benefitted from Iran's oil. What the US did not take into account was that even as it continued to be a friend of the Persian monarchy and benefitted from oil trade, Iran still dominated oil exports to the Soviet Union, its sales surpassing those of Libya, Iraq and Algeria.

In short, whereas the US saw politics and oil economics as being directly interrelated, the Middle Eastern oil producing countries viewed trade as an economic factor very different from political orientations. The 1970s and 80s may be decades ago, but the principles under which those countries operated have remained largely the same. After the first Gulf War, the general feeling in the US and elsewhere was that the US was going to have a greater advantage in the Middle East trade over other countries, including those in Europe. However, this was not the case. Whereas there were US companies that were advantaged in clinching contracts, especially in the fields of aerospace and the military, the overall trade balance remained unaltered.

In real figures, US exports to the Middle East in 1989, the year preceding the invasion of Kuwait by Iraq, amounted to $13.7 billion, while those of Europe to the same place totaled $40.2 billion. After the US kicked Iraq out of Kuwait and gained extra favor with many Gulf States, the trade position did not change much. Export volumes did indeed increase, of necessity, but the proportion of benefit in 1992, a year after Iraq was driven out of Kuwait, was not skewed in favor of the US. Exports from the US to the Middle East increased to $19.9 billion whereas those from Europe rose to $57.2 billion. Then in 2000, US exports to the region totaled $23 billion, whereas exports from Europe reached $63.7 billion.

In short, the US tries to position itself to benefit from oil resources in the Middle East as it increases its exports to the region, but that does not always give it a significant advantage over other countries.

# Chapter 3: Conspiracy Theory or Truth?

Once upon a time, countries with strong currencies pegged them against the value of gold. That was a good thing in so far as governments could not decide to increase the money in circulation haphazardly hence causing inflation that normally hurts the economy. Nevertheless, Britain decided to get its pound off the gold standard in 1931, and the US emulated it in 1933. Whatever parts of the gold standard system remained in the US' economy were abandoned under the leadership of President Richard Nixon in 1971.

Whether Nixon had good economic reasons to pull out the dollar from the gold standard or not, or whether he did it to divert attention from the political scandals associated with his administration may not be clearly known. Five people had been accused of having broken into the Democratic National Committee (DNC) offices during the campaign period and stolen documents, and the government had been accused of attempting to cover up the crime. It was later established that the Nixon administration had also gotten the FBI, the CIA, and even the IRS to harass political opponents.

Since these were allegations which, if proven, would have led to the impeachment of the president, it would not have been surprising for the president to try and divert attention from the political problems to a drastic financial move. President Nixon had assured the country that the US dollar would retain its value, but that did not happen.

However, initially it was promising that countries trading in oil used the US dollar as their medium of exchange, thus keeping the dollar in high demand and at a relatively stable value. In fact, the dollar came to be referred to as the petrodollar.

### *Conspiracy about Oil Producers Abandoning the Petrodollar*

Sometime in the 2000s, there was a conspiracy theory doing the rounds that major oil exporting countries would cease to use the US dollar as its trading currency, and in the thinking of many people, such a move would cause the value of the dollar to nosedive. It is even said that Saddam Hussein's decision to substitute the petrodollar with the Euro as the currency for Iraq's oil export was the real reason the US had invaded the country.

Even in 2009 when the US began to raise dust about Iran's nuclear program, word had it that the real reason was that Iran had threatened to abandon the use of the US dollar as well in its oil exports. In fact, there was an article in a London based paper, *The Independent,* which pointed out the existence of a conspiracy among big economies like China, Japan, Russia, France and the Arab nations, to cease the use of the US dollar in their oil transactions by 2018.

Of course such a rumor, whether it held any water or not, would cause some level of anxiety to people holding their financial resources in dollars, and more so to the US itself. The fear was that the US economy would collapse if the US currency ceased to be the petrodollar it has been for decades.

However, financial experts think the anxiety from fear of the dollar being abandoned in the major oil trade is unwarranted. They reckon the use of the US dollar in the oil trade was not a decision that was formally thought out for financial stability or any other financial reason in the first place. Rather, it was a convention that continued to develop over time, and any other currency can do just as well without destabilizing either the economy of the US or that of the world.

In any case, experts say, oil is just one item that is traded in US dollars, and the US would still have other products being traded internationally in dollars. As it were, many countries price their exports in US dollars, and they store their financial reserves in the same currency. So the alleged conspiracy that some countries would sabotage the US economy by switching from the petrodollar to the Euro or any other currency was given too much importance as far as the US economy was concerned.

In fact, if, as is frequently alleged, Muammar Gaddafi of Libya was fought and killed by US led forces for his campaign to have Africans trade in oil using the dinar, a new currency backed by gold, the fear behind it was misplaced. Libya, an African country known for its massive gold resources, estimated at around 150 tons, also encouraged governments in the Middle East to have their own currency to trade with in place of the petrodollar. From the financial analysts' point of view, many of the actions the US has taken in an attempt to safeguard use of its currency in oil trade have not been supported by sound financial reasoning. As far as experts are concerned, any currency could be used in place of the dollar, and that change on its own would not have much impact on the US economy.

## *Quest for Oil Has, Over the Years, Blurred US Vision*

It often turns out that every time the US has attacked another country, there is an ulterior motive, and the reason given to the public is just a smokescreen. In the case of Gaddafi who took over power in 1969 in a coup, albeit without bloodshed, the US did not raise a finger as he turned his reign into a dictatorship, and even as he traveled across the world allegedly sponsoring terror groups that destabilized legitimate governments.

At the time, the US wanted to safeguard its companies' share of oil resources in Libya, and did not want to provoke the wrath of their benefactor. Even when Gaddafi demanded a renegotiation of contracts with the American oil companies in Libya so that Libya became a partner with controlling power, America remained tame. The government must have taken the position that when it came to precious oil, half measure is better than no measure.

However, US' attitude towards Libya changed in April 1986, when Libya was implicated with the bombing of *The La Belle*, a disco club in Germany frequented by American soldiers. Whereas the West Berlin bombing caused three fatalities, President Reagan's retaliation that involved a bomb hit on Tripoli and Benghazi caused 37 fatalities. In September of the same year, Libya was again accused of being behind the hijacking of a plane, *Pan Am Flight 73*, where 20 lives were lost. Then there was the Lockerbie bombing of a French plane, *UTA Flight 772*, in 1989. Again, Gaddafi's regime was implicated.

In fact, as early as the 1970's, Libya had been involved in the support of the Irish Republican Army (IRA), a pro-socialist paramilitary group that had been outlawed as a terror organization in the UK, but which Gaddafi considered an ally in resisting Western imperialism.

Although it is a fact the first time America showed interest in the Middle East was in the 1800s, when President Thomas Jefferson sent American warships along the Tripoli shores to patrol the Mediterranean as protection against potential hijacking of American ships by pirates, it is clear the eagerness to take advantage of the oil resource soon became a guiding factor. In fact, US oil companies began to do business in Iraq, then Mesopotamia, in the 1910's, and the US has since strived to control the political dynamics of the region.

On the contrary, the US has little interest in countries that neither have oil nor political or economic influence on countries that have it. Why else was the US voice not heard as the IRA terrorized people in Ireland and its environs in the 1970s, before and after? Why was the US not bothered by the instability of Northern Ireland?

Distance could not have been the reason. After all, in addition to the US having taken the lead in recognizing far-off Israel in 1947, Americans retained their presence in the region and tried to get the Arab countries to recognize the new state. In the meantime, the US embarked on oil explorations in the region, even facilitating the establishment of the Arabian Pipeline, which enabled Americans to ferry oil from Saudi Arabia to the ports along the Mediterranean Sea. Notwithstanding the information disseminated through public media, whenever the US has engaged in military action against another country, the question of oil is always lurking somewhere.

## Chapter 4: US Use of Tariffs and Restrictions, and an Attempt to Weaken the TPP, to Influence the Geopolitics of the Region

US' tough stance on Syria, Iran or any other country that appears to be a threat to its economic, political and military influence in the Middle East is not a case isolated to the oil producing region alone. It can be seen in the way the Trump administration is behaving towards China as the Asian country continues to make its mark in international commerce.

While the ruling by the Permanent Court of Arbitration at The Hague (PCA) regarding China's occupation and construction in the South China Sea vindicated the US in the tough position it had taken against China, other threats by the Trump administration have raised eyebrows. The 2016 ruling was made in favor of the Philippines that had presented the case to the court following China's move to establish its own developments in the area, including an artificial island.

The US has always maintained a military presence in the region since the era of the Korean War of the 1950s, and the world has understood that to be a positive deterrent of possible military conflict among the neighboring countries, particularly between South and North Korea. However, it is apparent the main concern for the US is to monitor the major military and economic power that is China, not just to ensure the country does not encroach on the territories of smaller neighbors, but also to ensure China does not appear dominant in the eyes of the world. In fact, in March 2018, US and Japanese forces embarked on anti-submarine drills within the South China Sea, and the following month China reciprocated by putting on a display of its aircraft carrier and some submarines as its forces performed a three-day drill within the same region. In short, the US is very much interested in the geopolitics of Asia.

When it comes to the issue of tariffs, the Trump administration has threatened to impose heavy taxes on goods from countries with whom the US has trade deficits, and China is top on the US list. In fact, Trump has shown he is prepared to go beyond tariffs to curtail China's dominance in trade whenever possible, even as he reduces the trade deficit with the Asian powerhouse. It must, definitely, upset Trump to see that the trade deficit with China has continued to grow even during his administration.

In 2017, President Trump invoked his powers to safeguard national security, so as to block a Chinese company from acquiring a US company that is listed on the stock exchange. The government's move to block Canyon Bridge Fund from acquiring Lattice Semiconductor Corporation is a sign the US will not hesitate to influence trade matters in its favor, despite the country's continued advocacy for a free global market.

In March 2018, the US imposed tariffs and other restrictions on products from China worth $60 billion, and that move immediately caused uncertainty in the stock market. As the US tried to justify its action by citing some products such as cars on which China charges higher tariffs than the US, China took solace in the fact that the US is alone in this trade war, and it has not lured its allies into joining it.

Weeks down the line, in April, China did its bit to try and mitigate the impact of the new US tariffs, by imposing levies on US imports whose value is around $3 billion. It has not been lost on China that as the US imposes tariffs on steel and aluminum imports from China, those from South Korea and Canada have been exempt from similar levies. From the very beginning when the US threatened China with tariffs, the position of China has been that such a move was bound to hurt both economies. When the US declared China a competitor and went ahead to impose harsh tariffs, including a hike from 2.5% on imported Chinese cars to 25%, China accused the US of having a Cold-War mentality.

Some analysts in the US have termed the unilateral arm twisting by way of tariffs, the way the US has done to China, as being dangerous and a threat to the existing global trade system. Clearly, the US is bent on growing its economy at the expense of other countries, be it by influencing the oil market, or through coercion in other areas of trade. And in a good number of these cases, the US has a way of hiding behind the veil of national, regional or global security.

When it comes to Mexico, another country the Trump administration has been vocal about, trade between the South American country and the US has been in favor of Mexico, with the US continually suffering a deficit. In fact, as the US experienced a 7% trade deficit with China in 2017, the big economy experienced an 11% trade deficit with Mexico. In February 2018, Mexico stated it was determined to hit back at the US with its own tariffs on American goods if the US went ahead to impose tariffs on imports from Mexico.

In an amazing twist, when speaking to the press, White House spokeswoman, Sarah Sanders, said among the countries to be exempt from tariffs, particularly on aluminum and steel, were Canada and Mexico. And not surprisingly, the administration said the decision was based on security considerations. Before that statement, Mexico feared a 25% tariff imposition on steel products and a 10% tariff on aluminum products.

Clearly, it is mainly about self-serving power and influence when it comes to measures the US takes, whether in terms of military or economic action. In May 2018, the US declared the country had pulled out of the Iran nuclear accord. Not only was the US move upsetting to Iran, which has kept its side of the bargain since the accord was signed, but it was also unsettling to the other countries with whom the US had agreed to make a deal with Iran. Trump did not care that his country's European counterparts wanted the deal to remain in place, yet they are countries that the US collaborates with in other matters of global importance, including taking action under NATO. This may lead such countries to conclude that their partnership with the US, either bilaterally or within organizations such as NATO or the UN, is inconsequential.

## *European Countries Set to Salvage the Iran Accord*

Immediately following Trump's announcement about US withdrawal from the Iran deal, the European countries, led by France, began to consult to see how to salvage the deal with Iran. In fact, France was categorical that the deal still remained, and the only change that has happened is that the US is no longer part of it. In their efforts, the European countries even talked directly with the Tehran administration.

President Macron of France, for instance, declared to Iran that his administration was committed to honoring all aspects of the accord as agreed, and he hoped Iran would do likewise. Other countries that echoed the sentiments of France included Germany, Belgium, UK, China and Russia. If things continue in this manner, it looks like the US might end up isolating itself as it endeavors to isolate others.

The only country that seems to be celebrating is Israel. After all, in the run up to the US withdrawal from the Iran nuclear deal, Prime

Minister Netanyahu had been making subtle media campaigns against the Iran deal, including one memorable presentation he made from Israel in English as opposed to his usual mode of communication, Hebrew.

The effect of the US' withdrawal from the Iran deal is yet to be seen and felt, but in addition to the feeling among some Americans that their promises as a country, even when official, will no longer be taken seriously by other nations, there was anxiety following Trump's announcement, concerning how Iran might react. Nevertheless, Trump and Netanyahu believe the deal was an unwarranted reward to Iran.

In fact, US withdrawal elicited fear that Iran might now go rogue without reservations, because without the deal the country would not have much, if anything, to lose. However, President Hassan Rouhani of Iran has been cooperative, and he has even instructed his diplomats to enter into discussions with the other partners in the accord with a view to salvaging the agreement. Of course, things are not all rosy. US withdrawal from the Iran deal has revived old problems for Rouhani who is a moderate, from hardliners who have never trusted a deal with the West, and others who would rather Iran remained unaccountable to anyone like North Korea. In fact, Ayatollah Ali Khamenei, Iran's Supreme Leader, has said even the European countries in the deal cannot be trusted to keep their side of the bargain either. Khamenei served as Iran's third president from 1981 to 1989.

Unfortunately, US' selfishness does not spare even friends. With the accord signed during the Obama administration, some countries that formerly had nothing to do with Iran began to trade with the pariah country. If the accord is broken, those countries with companies engaged in business with Iran will be adversely affected, and the economies back home cannot be spared either. Airbus is such an entity that would be affected. It is a European consortium that won a contract in 2016 to supply Iran Air with 100 planes, and that contract was worth $19 billion. Total of France also has a business contract with Iran that is worth $2 billion, and it involves development of an oil field meant to serve both Iran and Qatar.

Incidentally, an insider was reported to have revealed anonymously that withdrawal of such businesses from Iran was actually the Trump administration's deliberate intention. Even if it were a good way of keeping the region safer, it would still be inconsiderate for the US to cause the breaking of the accord in such a manner. As a businessperson, Trump, obviously, understands the consequences of breaking a business contract, the capital input involved even to initiate the business venture especially away from home, and such other aspects of business. So the reality is that he simply does not care who loses, friend or foe, as long as the Republican Party, Israel and the rest of the world see him as a tough president.

Unfortunately, President Trump's actions do not seem to portray him as a tough president, probably because of the diverse parties he affects in a negative way. Instead, he appears somewhat erratic. One cannot help but wonder if he had considered the impact on Boeing and the US economy, when the US Company loses $20 billion in contracts won in Iran after the accord, not to mention the massive incidental costs.

As things stand, US companies might be the only ones to lose after the other signatories to the Iran deal salvage the accord. If Trump's idea was to make the world see who calls the shots where it matters, his actions might backfire on him. When he got the US out of the TPP, all the other eleven countries remained firmly put, and the agreements remained as discussed, only being amended to factor in US exit. Now the US has withdrawn from the Iran accord, and the other partners have remained steadfast.

With the developments that have taken place within a few months involving foreign policy and international relations, the US has now become a country to watch, and unfortunately, with some concern. Trump's administration has rubbed China the wrong way through impromptu tariffs, done the same to Iran by withdrawing the US from the nuclear accord, disappointed its partners along the Pacific through US withdrawal from the TPP, irked Russia by interfering in the Syria conflict, and treated European allies in the Iran deal with disdain.

Could the US be under the illusion the country will not require the cooperation of other countries any time in the future? Or is the administration taking its old friends for granted as it seeks a relationship with North Korea? For now, one can only wait to see how things turn out for both the US and the affected countries.

### *The Potential of the TPP Cannot Be Ignored*

One thing is clear. The US might talk tough on Mexico, including the threat to build a physical wall between the two countries, but the administration realizes the power of a working economic block. Mexico is one of the twelve countries that make up the Trans-Pacific Partnership (TPP), which had not been formerly signed by the time Trump took office as US president. The other member countries are Japan, Peru, Canada, Malaysia, Australia, Brunei, New Zealand, Chile, Singapore and Vietnam, and under the Obama administration, the US was one of them.

President Trump always saw the position of the US in the TPP as a burden to the country, the same way he viewed US position in organizations such as the UN. In fact, in his view, such a partnership would not hold or have any influence without the participation of the US. The US has since pulled out of the proposed TPP. It must have been a surprise, therefore, when in January 2018, the Australian Prime Minister, Malcolm Turnbull, announced the agreement among the eleven remaining partners to forge ahead, and in March 2018 when the TPP agreement was formerly signed in Chile.

With the TPP working on streamlining and strengthening trade among the member countries, and bringing down tariffs as well, the US must have realized that a hike in tariffs on Mexico would be self defeating. Mexico would, very likely, divert its affected exports to the TPP countries and then impose retaliatory tariffs on US goods, in which case the US would be the net loser.

The members of the TPP expressed their dislike for the kind of protectionism the Trump administration was trying to exercise, saying they were determined to advance global trade. They renegotiated the original pact that involved twelve countries, and renamed their organization that now comprises eleven countries, *Comprehensive and Progressive Trans-Pacific Partnership* (CPTPP). In January 2018 when Turnbull announced the resolve by the TPP's remaining member countries, he pointed out that already a quarter of their products were sold within the member countries.

The move by the eleven countries means there are countries that have read through the US foreign policy and seen some dishonesty in it, and have decided to resist its influence which would otherwise have the US prospering at their expense. In fact, countries like Australia are looking for more ways than one to grow their economy. Already, the administration of Prime Minister Turnbull is discussing with the UK to see how they can forge a trade partnership post Brexit. For instance, while the UK would be happy to export services, such as banking services, to Australia, the latter would be glad to export agricultural products to the UK.

And just as Russia's presence in the Syrian conflict neutralizes US influence in the outcome, economic cooperation among countries in the neighborhood of the US is set to neutralize US influence in the region. In fact, by making the US a member of the TPP, the Obama administration saw a genteel way that could potentially suppress China's dominance in the region. Now that the US has opted out, the country has a lone fight to pick with China, a country that has already stretched its economic tentacles across the globe, including in Africa. Needless to say, countries that have strong economic ties are likely to be sympathetic to one another politically. Hence the geopolitics of the region is bound to, inevitably, change.

# Chapter 5: 2018 Attack on Syria's Chemical weapons Manufacturing Plants and Assad's Regime

When in April 2018 the US, aided by its two allies, proceeded to strike Syria with missiles, it took the risk of provoking Russia into retaliation. Such retaliation could have taken any form, including a direct shoot-out between Russian soldiers and those of the US or its allies. Whereas that possibility did not occur, the attack is likely to have given Russia food for thought, and it is not easy to tell how Putin's regime might react if there is a similar incident. Still, it is understandable why the two big military powers may not wish to enter into direct confrontation with each other, especially a military conflict that might escalate to World War III.

Right now, each of these big countries justifies its presence in Syria as an attempt to crush the Islamic terrorist groups. As for Bashar-al-Assad, his efforts are geared towards suppressing opposition to his government wherever that opposition may come from, and since he has his external supporters like Iran and Turkey, Syria has become a very crowded field of fighters. The situation becomes even more complicated when one considers the reality that each one group represented in Syria has its selfish interest in influencing matters in the region. Turkey initially got involved to fight ISIS, like some other players, whereas Kurds, who have been problematic to Turkey, make up a good part of the group fighting the Assad regime. As it were, Turkey is already doing its own battle in Northern Syria in an attempt to disable groups allied to the infamous Kurdish PKK.

### *Russia Threatens To Counter US Attacks*

As President Trump continued to issue threats against Syria, Russia's ambassador to Lebanon expressly said that any missiles targeting Syria would, most probably, be shot down, giving the impression that Russia was ready to defend Syria against the US and not just against anti-government rebels. President Putin himself warned in the wake of President Trump's threats to Syria that consequences of the gravest magnitude would follow if America took military action against Syria. He even labeled the allegations of a chemical attack, fake news.

Russia has been helping President Bashar-al-Assad's regime to crush its own Syrian rebels, and it has even used warplanes for that purpose. In addition, Russia has also offered manpower to fight the anti-government forces on the ground, although the Putin regime speaks of them as mercenaries.

The situation in Syria is a tricky one, and it has not just become so with the alleged use of chemical weapons by Assad. It is said there are around 2,000 US soldiers in the country, and their role is to offer support to the forces fighting the Islamic State in Iraq and Syria (ISIS), mainly in form of advice to the Syrian Defense Forces. In short, the US is in Syria under the mantle of fighting terrorists for the sake of world peace. Yet, the aspect of the US presence being a proxy war with Russia is not lost on observers.

In February, the so-called mercenaries attacked a US base, and whereas the spokesperson for the United States Central Command, Colonel Ryan Dillon, could not confirm the number of deaths caused to the Russian backed fighters, he did admit his group had been attacked by pro-Assad fighters. Other sources said as many as a hundred soldiers contracted by Russia were killed. Nevertheless, Colonel Dillon said that Russian officials had promised to desist from attacking the US-led coalition forces within Syria.

### As The US Claims Success in Its Missile Attack, Russia Gives an Image of an Ineffective Provocation

From the US side, it was reported that the missiles deployed by the US and its allies hit its three targets, which they believed had something to do with chemical weapons. However, the Russians' side says six airbases were targets of the missile attacks, and they included al-Dumayr military airport, Shayrat airbase, and another airbase close to Homs.

Nevertheless, one point Russia tried to highlight was the ineffectiveness of the attack, saying the US-led forces had launched a total of 103 missiles, but more than two-thirds of them were intercepted by Syria, the actual number of those intercepted being 71. Col Gen Sergei Rudskoi, a Russian military officer, said the damage done on Syrian military facilities was minimal, and the strikes caused no casualties.

And as the US tries to give the impression the anti-missile systems Russia has provided to Syria are old or just short-range and therefore not that good, what comes to mind is the 2017 missile attack on Syria's Shayrat airbase by the US in 2017, when Syria was able to launch missiles against its rebels only hours after the US strike. In short, none of these reports can be taken at face value, as each side does its best to reflect the image of power, tact and invincibility.

## The US and its Allies Broke UN Protocol

In a case where the US and European countries feel justified to attack another country, whether it is to safeguard the sovereignty of another country or such other noble act, the normal procedure is to get authorization from the UN Security Council or to act as the *North Atlantic Treaty Organization* (NATO).

This did not happen when the US, Britain and France launched missiles in April 2018. When the issue of Syria was brought up for consideration in an emergency meeting of the UN Security Council set after the alleged April chemical attack, the meeting ended up being more of a showdown between Russia and the US, each of them arguing in a contrary direction to the other. In fact, each had its own drafts they hoped the council would pass, but none of them was accepted. Instead, it was agreed a team of investigators would be sent to verify if, in actual fact, chemical weapons had been used in Syria on April 7, 2018 as alleged.

The US and its allies, Britain and France, who happen to be permanent members of the Council, proceeded to launch missiles into Syria in an attempt to cripple certain facilities in the country, even before the UN investigators had begun their work. This is one instance that shows President Trump still believes the international organization is ineffective and inconsequential. As the US and its allies ignore UN protocol, they are confident there is no feasible punitive measure the international body can take against them. All along, the US has longed to see the regime of President Assad crumble and new leadership taking over, but economic sanctions against Syria have not worked.

It is also true that the Trump administration has been opposed to the Iran nuclear deal sealed during the Obama administration, and still considers Iran dangerous and a threat to US interest. Now that Iran has its soldiers on the ground in Syria helping to keep Assad in power, Trump may have found it a good time to hit Iranians and weaken Iran's military power as the US coalition deals with the Syria chemical issue.

On the domestic front, the April 14 attack may be seen by Americans as confirmation that the existence of the UN is an unnecessary expense as Trump told them during the 2016 presidential campaigns. After all, Trump has led his allies, UK and France, to take the action he deemed appropriate, despite lack of consensus at the UN and no official UN resolution.

It is also telling that the Trump administration has undermined the UN Security Council under the watch of John Bolton, the hawkish national security advisor whom Trump appointed in March 2018 to replace the more moderate, H.R. McMaster. While Bolton may not have been the decision maker, he is likely to have given affirmation to President Trump's suggestion to strike Syria irrespective of what anyone else thought, including the UN.

It is obvious the US has been emboldened by the fact that no punitive measures have been taken against the administration whenever it has ignored the UN Charter in the past. A case in point is the 2003 invasion of Iraq, which the former UN Secretary General, Kofi Annan, has said was not sanctioned by the UN. In fact, when the discussions were ongoing, he had clearly told the US and its allies that it would be illegal for them to proceed with the invasion without the UN passing a resolution to that effect.

Still, the US might try to justify its actions as a moral obligation, and allege its interventions have been to stop carnage of civilians by governments notorious of using chemical weapons to suppress opposition. Of course, this premise would not hold in the case of Iraq where it has been established the regime of Saddam Hussein had no stocks of weapons of mass destruction (WMD), but the argument could be made in the case of Syria. The US may have good reason to believe the Assad regime still has stockpiles of chemical weapons, especially considering that the regime's most vocal advocate in this matter has been Russia, a military and political opponent of the US. Russia has been supporting Syria militarily, and there is no reason why Syria would not reciprocate and give Russia access to WMDs if ever Russia wanted them.

It is important to note that Syria, just like North Korea, has not ratified the Chemical Weapons Convention (CWC) that came into force in 1997. However, the country, which in recent years has severally been accused of using chemical weapons on its people, is a signatory to the 1925 Geneva Protocol that prohibits countries from using chemical weapons. Most likely, the US is convinced that Syria still has stockpiles of chemical weapons and is probably producing more, and that is probably the reason the administration did not wish to wait for the UN to formally send a team of inspectors.

Even if the UN Security Council had given a go-ahead to the US and its allies to hit Syria with missiles, it is likely the body would have limited the strikes to specific locations that the investigators had found evidence of chemical weapons' presence; if they actually found any. In short, a go-ahead for an attack would be based on the findings of an UN-sanctioned investigation. Yet the US might have its own intelligence pointing elsewhere in the country and it wanted to ensure it attacked those areas as well. In August 2013, following proof found by members of the *Organization for the Prohibition of Chemical Weapons* (OPCW) that Assad's regime had used Sarin, a chemical weapon, and spread it through surface to surface rockets to specific areas of the country, President Obama sought authority from Congress to attack Syria.

However, Russia intervened to save Syria, convincing Assad's regime to accept to get rid of its chemical weapons. Although chemical weapons were destroyed in Syria in October 2013 under the supervision of the OPCW, some information from people who know President Assad better has it he would never relinquish all his stockpiles of chemical weapons. One such person is a former Syrian general who had an interview with CNN's Christiane Amanpour, and who said he had defected because he could not bring himself to use chemical weapons as required of him by the regime. He said that in his assessment, President Bashar-al-Assad would never relinquish his entire stocks of chemical weapons.

In short, it is likely the US has adopted the principle of the "end justifying the means", and has taken the position it is better to break international protocol than let a ruthless dictator continue to perpetrate evil against his people and be a threat to neighbors. Still, it is not clear how much the US-organized strikes accomplished, and only future activities in Syria will tell if Assad still has chemical WMDs.

## *Probably There Is Indication Syria Has A Nuclear Program*

There is still another angle the US and its allies might have considered with the Syrian case. The world has been concerned about the regime's use of chemical weapons, and even in April 2018 when there were signs such chemicals had affected people in Syria, Assad knew credible images would be splashed across the globe. Suppose the use of chemicals as weapons is President's Assad's ploy to divert attention from a nuclear program he has already developed? That could be a possibility the US has been considering.

After all, Syria has been suspected of secretly trying to develop nuclear weapons, following in the footsteps of Iran and Libya. Even Iraq had been accused of secretly initiating a nuclear program sometime before the US entered into a confrontation with Saddam Hussein's regime in the 1991 Gulf War. Such a concern by the US would not be unwarranted considering North Korea has continued to develop nuclear weapons and has even owned up to it, and no resolution has ever been passed at international level to invade the small country militarily. In fact, in President Kim Jong Un's 2018 New Year address, he bragged that North

Korea's nuclear weapons have the capacity to reach any part of the US mainland.

As for Assad, he is aware that what has been hurting the regime of Kim Jong Un are economic sanctions and not the noise the US and other countries have been making against it. As such, Assad might be emboldened by the fact that Russia is on his side and would not let his regime crumble under economic sanctions. On the overall, the US must have realized no official channels would lead to elimination of Assad's unconventional lethal weapons, and hence Trump decided to follow his own plan of hitting Syria at his own time, while targeting areas of his own choosing.

### *Syria Conflict Unlikely to Trigger WWIII*

Unless something out of the ordinary happens, the Syria case is unlikely to lead to World War III. For one, the US would like to avoid such an eventuality, because the administration does not know for certain what is practically going on within Syria. At the same time, US forces do not know enough about the geographical region.

The situation with Syria is intricate, and for the years the civil war has been raging, many interested parties have engaged in the mess. There are now the Assad soldiers, Russian soldiers, Iranian soldiers, Russia-backed mercenaries, Syrian rebels, Turkish soldiers, clandestine groups like the Hezbollah, Turkish Kurds, ISIS, and many other varied elements on the ground. It would be too costly, particularly in terms of human life, if the US were to initiate a massive war, where it is not easy to distinguish an ally from an enemy, know who to trust and who to guard against, and to know exactly the location of each of those entities.

The fact that the US may not know much about the region geographically as well as the attitudes of different people involved could jeopardize the forces' ground operations. The forces would actually be disadvantaged when dealing with logistics. Besides, Russia is the last country the US would like to go to war with, and there is no way a war could escalate to WWIII and leave Russia out of it. For now, even experts, exemplified by Didier Leroy, a Brussels University assistant professor, are of the opinion a big war involving Russia and the US is unlikely, although there are, certainly, tensions between the two big world powers.

According to Leroy, who also does research at the *Royal Institute of Defense* in Belgium, President Trump hardly understands the geopolitics of the region, implying he is unlikely to get involved in the conflict at a more complex level.

Logistics and attitudes aside, no country today is eager to enter into a massive war, and this may explain why leaders of super powers have mastered the craft of "talking tough". They would rather use words or threats as deterrent of bad behavior than engage in a war of armaments. All countries that were involved in the two World Wars, especially WWII where bombs were used, realized that going to war with one another is the surest way for human beings to annihilate themselves. Some people have termed it *Mutually Assured Destruction* (MAD), a term that seems appropriate considering the experience of the two World Wars.

In WWI when the alliance of Germany, Bulgaria, Austria-Hungary and the Ottoman Empire, otherwise known as the *Central Powers*, fought against the alliance comprising France, the UK and Russia, under the banner of the *Triple Entente*, assisted by Canada, Australia, the US, New Zealand, Greece, India,

Italy, Serbia and South Africa to become simply the Allied Countries, total damage was massive. By the time the war ended, the Central Powers had lost 4.02 million lives in military casualties and over 5.2 million in civilian casualties, while the Allied Countries had lost 5.7 million lives in military casualties and 3.67 million in civilian casualties.

Injuries totaled 8.42 million and 12.8 million for the Central Powers and Allied Countries respectively. There was also massive destruction of property on both sides, and the entire war cost in excess of $186 billion. Such magnitude of fatalities and destruction is certainly mind boggling, and it is enough to keep countries from contemplating war. The impact of WWII is also not any consolation, as death and casualty figures ran into tens of millions, and destruction was also colossal.

Massive war vibes may rent the air whenever there are conflicts like the one based in Syria, but countries tend to have history as a reality check. In fact, the Syrian situation is not the first to invoke fears of WWIII. There was the 1962 Cuba missile crisis, which brought the US and the Soviet Union to near combat; the false alarm of 1983 where the US received warning of an impending attack by the Soviet Union only to be certified false; and even the 1999 Kosovo War where both super powers, Russia and the US, were actively involved, complete with soldiers on the ground. On the overall, therefore, one can consider the world largely safe, but hope that world leaders will not let their personal egos or the desire for dominance override caution.

# *Chapter 6:* America Losing World's Superpower Status Fast

With the world becoming a global village, many countries are having easy access to markets, technology and skills that only the world superpowers used to have access to some years back. For example, for some decades after WWII, the US would 'poach' scientists from smaller countries like Israel and Germany to help with innovation, but today there is largely free movement of skilled labor across the world. Besides, the internet has broken many information barriers and made knowledge accessible to virtually everyone. In short, in many of the fields the US led, it now has serious competitors.

When it comes to military skill and equipment, Russia and China feel they are equals with the US, and they are not afraid to display this attitude publicly; sometimes taunting the US administration when it talks tough. Most importantly, though, is the fact that in the present day, military prowess alone does not give a country a big advantage over others when it comes to gauging the level of superpower status. In any case, as has already been mentioned elsewhere in this book, the entire world is wary of a WWIII and there is no longer any country eager to go to war. What, then, is the best measure of a country's superpower status?

Today countries respect one another on the basis of economic status as well as level of technology. The country that others look up to is the one whose economy is strong, growing, and is showing signs of stability; and also one whose level of technology surpasses that of the other countries. When it comes to technology, Japan appears to be gearing itself to lead internationally. Incidentally, technology is a key economic driver today, and so Japan is on its way to making a mark on the global scene also economically.

There are many large technology companies in Japan, and analysts cannot fail but find a link between that fact and Japan's sustained economic growth. What is notable too is the fact that Japan is in the process of creating the most powerful computer in the world, to overtake the US that has been in the lead after overtaking China that was in the lead before that.

America's most powerful computer is named Summit, and it was credited with the global lead in June 2018. The peak performance of this supercomputer is 122.3 petaflops, whereas the performance of the one Japan has in the pipeline is set to be 130 petaflops. In other words, Japan is about to lead the world in technological advancement, with its supercomputer having capacity to process 130 quadrillion calculations per second.

Japan used to be known for its technological advancements when very few people in the workplace were computer literate, and then it was overtaken by the US that is home to Google and Apple, and China as well. Now the country is putting its focus back to the field of technology with the intention of dethroning its two biggest competitors. Among the areas Japan is putting heavy investment in are robotics and renewable energy. In fact the reason the new supercomputer is set to be superfast is not just to have Japan take the crown for the most powerful computer, but more so to help the country increase its innovation capacity in the areas of medical diagnostics, robotics, artificial intelligence and creation of driverless cars. In this regard, Prime Minister Abe has called for enhanced cooperation between the country's public and private sectors.

Once such cooperation is achieved, the country may hasten to reach its goal of surpassing other leading countries in technological achievements. The country specifically plans on beating the US in AI, developing programs that are more advanced than Google's DeepMind AI Program that has proven to have capacity to beat a professional player of the Go board game.

From an economic standpoint, Japan's plan, once its supercomputer is completed, is to allow private corporations to use it at a fee, meaning the country is going to raise some revenue from the supercomputer even as it facilitates research and other important processes. Currently, many corporations in the country requiring high-tech processing outsource the services from Google and Microsoft, hence promoting the US economy. In short, Japan intends to soon become self sufficient in technology, and the country is likely to begin exporting technological services to neighboring countries, hence boosting its economy.

India itself is on an economic rise and not only because its economic growth has been consistently rising – surpassing 7% in 2018 – but also because the country is becoming all the more friendly to foreign investors.

## *How Empires Crumble*

A country may dominate the world in a certain sector, but there is no guarantee it will remain in the lead forever. Such a country has to be prepared to face challenges that come with changing times, as well as competition and threats that come with new alliances.

Just for example, there was a time when the US was so powerful militarily and economically that its word to leaders of developing nations was taken as law. They implemented policy changes the way the US wanted done, lest Big Brother withdrew much needed funds that came in form of loans and grants. Now developing nations are building multi-billion dollar infrastructure courtesy of China's financial and technical assistance, and advancing their citizen's technological skills courtesy of countries like Japan. In addition, US military threats to intimidate countries no longer makes them shudder the way terrorism does. In short, whatever power the US had over most of the world has slowly but gradually been eroding.

For an empire to survive, it must have something it can hold above its subjects, and in the case of the US, either there are other countries that have caught up with the big power, or its threats have become invalid, courtesy of altered world dynamics. Even in history there are good examples of empires that people watched in awe as they rose in power and influence, but then they ended up breaking into fragments as power dynamics changed. Such empires include the Mongolian Empire, the Aztec Empire and the British Empire.

### The Mongolian Empire

The Mongolian empire is an intriguing example, especially because its expansion was speedy and seemingly definitive, yet it did it not take much external pressure for it to disintegrate. Experts say the Mongolian empire expanded very fast by killing millions of people and destroying their cities, and the land they captured within 25 years, stretching from the Pacific Ocean to the Danube River, was more than the Roman Empire gained in 400 years. Yet that empire that was led by the family of Genghis Khan no longer exists. If its fall can be described in one word, self-destruction would suffice.

Fragmentation began when Genghis Khan's sons began to fight over leadership succession, and with divergent self-interests, the empire's ability to protect itself from outside threat began to diminish. Now there is the Republican Party in the US having problems identifying a candidate they unanimously have faith in, as seen in the 2016 presidential elections, much of the voting being done on other basis than knowledge of the candidate's abilities. Though the party has remained united against the opposition, which is dominated by the Democratic Party, the intermittent internal political wrangles have given the world the image of a country striving to keep its house in order. So, in the world's eyes, the US has too much on its plate internally to threaten or influence any outsider.

<u>*The Aztec Empire*</u>

The Aztec Empire, initially comprised three city states of Mexico, Tenochtitlan, Texcoco, and Tlacopan, but it later incorporated most of central Mexico and other regions further away, including Belize, the northern part of Costa Rica, El Salvador, Nicaragua, Honduras and Guatemala. This empire lasted almost a century – from 1428 to 1521 – and there were a number of challenges causing concern before the empire's collapse.

Among the main challenges was disease, with the Spanish explorers coming in with new illnesses such as the deadly smallpox that made the natives significantly weak. Another one was the aspect of misunderstanding emanating from the natives' religious beliefs. On the arrival of Hernan Cortes, a conquistador who had abandoned a Cuban expedition he had been on, Montezuma II who was then the Aztec emperor mistook him for God, and hence put his guard down. Conquistador means conqueror, and some of those conquistadors who entered Mexico during the Aztec empire happened to be soldiers.

Of course the Spanish, who later decidedly fought the Aztecs, had superior weapons that included cannons, but the ultimate collapse of the Aztec empire came when the natives forged an alliance with the Spanish conquistadores to wage a war against the Aztecs. Today, many leaders, including those of the Western world, are being increasingly disillusioned by America's policies in trade, immigration and more; and more so the country's antagonistic stance on issues of global concern like climate change.

Formation of alliances that do not have America as part of them may just be the last nail in the coffin with respect to US' status as a superpower. For instance, the US was quick to withdraw from the proposed TPP when Donald Trump became US President, but contrary to some presumption that the initiative would become a non-starter without the membership of the US, the eleven remaining members proceeded to complete the signing of the TPP agreement; only changing the name to CPTPP.

Later on when the US disowned the Iran nuclear deal, the European partners who had entered into the agreement together with the US during the presidency of Barrack Obama remained steadfast, and as far as Iran and the rest of the world is concerned, the Iran deal is still valid.

In the meantime, the US is befriending North Korea with nothing tangible to show as the pariah country's goodwill, and the world at large is appalled. If polarization continues internally around the issue of immigration, the US will have a lot of firefighting to do both on the domestic and foreign fronts, and that just goes against the country's efforts to retain its superpower status.

The British Empire was at some point in history the greatest world superpower, having begun its expansion in the 16th century. In fact, by 1921, the empire covered a quarter of the world's land, and by extension had dominion over its inhabitants. However, today, having released Hong Kong to China in 1997, the British Empire is only left with a few islands away from the UK and a claim to some area in the Antarctic.

Just like many of the other fallen empires, the defeat of the British came about when different groups, dissatisfied with the extremities of the British which included arbitrary executions of the natives, forged alliances with the common goal of frustrating and ultimately ending British sovereignty over them. America, which also felt the brunt of the British rule, led the way when natives joined forces with France and other powers to wage the American Revolutionary War that lasted from 1765 to 1783. In Africa, where the British had done a good job of exacerbating tribal divisions, different groups still found a way to form alliances and to frustrate British rule, which culminated with the colonies gaining their independence. The case was not much different in India that gained its independence from Britain in 1947.

### *Silk Road Revival Could be the Ultimate Game Changer*

China has begun a grand initiative to revive the Silk Road, and President Xi Jinping's effort to involve other countries seems to have given the initiative a big boost. China officially set off the program in May 2017 when it held a forum in Beijing dubbed One Belt, One Road, where around 60 countries were represented.

The Silk Road is an ancient trade route that connected China via land and sea to the continents of Africa and Europe, and also to the rest of Asia, and if its revival becomes a success, trillions of dollars will be generated through tourism and other forms of trade. A notable fact is that the 65 countries that have shown interest in being part of the China-led initiative constitute 60% of the world's population, and they represent a third of the world's gross domestic product (GDP).

The trade cooperation that is bound to be born is likely to have far reaching implications, not least among them initiating new political alignments. As Pakistani Prime Minister, Mian

Muhammad Nawaz Sharif noted as he affirmed his support for OBOR, what drives present day politics is economics. This fact cannot have been lost on the US, as at the last minute the administration decided to send a representative to the OBOR forum. Of course, there may have been other factors that influenced US' decision to attend the big forum, such as the fact that the attendees included both friends and foes of the US, and the absence of US representation would not have made any impact on anyone.

Among US nemeses who were represented at the forum were Iran and North Korea, and Russia's president appeared in person. America's European friends were also represented, including France, Germany and the UK.

The initiative to revive the Silk Road is said to be the world's most ambitious ever, as it even beats the US Marshall Plan that set the way for the reconstruction of Europe after the destruction done in WWII. When the OBOR forum was held, 130 countries were represented with 29 heads of countries in attendance, and that gave China the affirmation it may have needed that its economic plan was feasible.

According to Professor Hugh White, who expressed his views on the East Asia Forum, China's plan is to establish its position in the middle of the world's supply and manufacturing networks. Other analysts see the initiative by China as an attempt to integrate economies across Asia, Africa and Europe through efficient networks of transport and communication, and consequently redefining the world's 21st century economy. Without being spelt out, the initiative might just ebb the US out of the global economic equation, and, inevitably, its politics would be of little consequence to the rest of the world.

Some years ago, initiatives of a global magnitude were unlikely to succeed without US backing, and the fact that China is receiving positive signals from world bodies without having to solicit the backing of the US or any other superpower says a lot about the changing global dynamics. Already China's initiative has elicited interest from the United Nations (UN), World Bank, as well as the International Monetary Fund (IMF).

### *China Commits US$ Billions to the OBOR Initiative*

The OBOR initiative is estimated to be a US$4 trillion program, and there are already financiers ready to begin releasing funds to support it. The fact that the US is not one of those financiers, at least directly, means the administration has no influence on the course the initiative takes.

China has led the way by setting aside US$890 billion for particular 900 projects within the initiative, and there is some more US$40 billion it has set aside as China's Silk Road infrastructure fund. In addition, New Development Bank (NDB) based in Shanghai has committed to release US$50 billion for the project. In the build up to the OBOR forum, China's president announced his country would put more money into the Silk Road Fund, to the tune of 100 billion yuan, even as the China Development Bank and the Export and Import Bank of China committed to release 250 billion yuan and 130 billion yuan to the initiative respectively. The amount of money other Chinese banks have committed to support the Silk Road initiative total 300 billion yuan.

With this kind of financial commitment by China, other stakeholders are likely to have faith in the initiative and be prepared to give their support. International organizations are likely to be influenced into adding more financing as need arises, seeing how much China is committed to spending on the project. Since 2013 when China began to invest in economies along the Silk Road, the country has reaped close to US$1.1 billion in form of taxes, and this goes to show the kind of potential the initiative portends. In fact, its potential can only be measured in terms of trillions of dollars.

Although President Xi Jinping has denied his country's ambitious initiative is political and says it is solely economic, analysts say it is China's intention to expand its strategic as well as political influence at the expense of America. Another analyst by the name of Ankit Panda, while commenting for The Diplomat said that OBOR is actually about the global order and where China stands in that order, meaning that in a covert way, the US could find itself on the periphery of the world's stage.

### *India's Youthful Workforce Set to Last Decades*

There may not be as much fuss being made about India as there is about China, but India, whose annual economic growth rate has been impressive at between 5% and 6% for several years now, has an edge over some other contenders to superpower status. According to world's known consultancy firm, Deloitte LLP, India has the advantage of a youthful workforce.

While China will have to contend with an increased aging population, expected to rise from 365 million to ½ billion by 2027, India's age curve will be moving to the opposite direction. India's workforce is expected to rise from 885 million to 1.08 billion within the next two decades and continue rising for around 50yrs. As at 2015, the country's population not beyond 35yrs of age constituted 65% of the entire country's population, meaning that India has a rich pool from where to generate a strong workforce for the next several decades.

Considering the country is also fast advancing in technology, it means it might have fewer economic challenges than other countries that have recently been performing well economically. According to Deloitte, countries with an aging populace, besides China whose over 65yr olds will constitute a third of the world's aging population, include New Zealand, South Korea, Hong Kong, Singapore, Taiwan and Thailand. Japan has already been experiencing the challenge of an aging population, and Australia is said to be on that trend as well.

There has been renewed hope for India's economic prosperity since Prime Minister Narendra Modi rose to power in 2014. His promise to reform the government and jumpstart the economy gave hope to the millions of hardworking Indians, and got the world considering the country's potential for superpower status.

It was apparent President Barrack Obama could see India's potential as a strategic economic partner as he paid the country a 3-day visit at the beginning of 2015. After all, India is the world's biggest democracy and it neighbors China whose mode of politics the US abhors. India is, therefore, better placed to enjoy economic benefits from liaisons with the West, unlike China whose economic domination is seen as a threat, not only in economic terms but also in politics.

According to the IMF, India has surpassed Japan as the third biggest economy in the world. This, coupled with the country's progression towards a real free market as promised by Prime Minister Modi, as well as a highly productive workforce, makes the country well poised for great economic success.

### *India's Commitment to Enhance Infrastructure*

It is also worth noting that India embraces politics of cooperation as opposed to isolation, an attitude that enables the country to have more friends than foes. In an effort to improve the country's infrastructure, Prime Minister Modi secured an infrastructure investment of US$20 billion from China. The investment is not only expected to improve the country's transport system, but also improve the stability of water supply to the people and extend electricity and technology connectivity to more areas of the country.

Modi is keen on improving the country's national infrastructure, and to this end, he has committed to spending US$800 billion. He sees the potential of an improved infrastructure to help the country attain an economic growth rate of 7%. Prime Minister Modi's targets seem quite achievable, considering that almost every country wants India as a partner, not only because it has a big consumer market, but also because the country does not seem to be anyone's threat politically.

### *India is Highly Sought for Global Partnership*

Modi also appreciates the benefits that come with regional and international cooperation, and in that regard he has extended a hand of cooperation not only to the US but also to Russia and Japan. These countries, especially the big economies, do not want India's cooperation solely for economic reasons, but also to neutralize each other's influence in the region. Russia's economy, for example, has taken a beating from sanctions imposed by the West some years back, and fluctuating oil prices have not exactly helped the country's economy. As for the US, although it would be happy to expand its bilateral trade with India that hit US$95 billion in 2013, another issue that is just as important is forging an alliance with India in order to outbalance China's overall influence in the region.

It is safe to say, a country that is being highly sought by others for their economic or political success, and has room to accept or reject certain alliances, has real potential to become a superpower. In the case of India, though it is being cordial with everyone, it will only commit to those alliances that will propel it to the highest stature possible, both economically and politically.

# Chapter 7: More than Military Might Needed to Become a Super Power

To be and remain a superpower, it is important for a country to have capacity to ward off external aggression and also protect other countries that may be weaker. That is the position the US has been in for many years, with its heavy military might. For example, the projection for the number of active duty armed forces personnel for 2017 was around 1.3 million, while close to a million made up the overall reserve component. Even if the number exceeded these figures, the overall would still be less than 3 million in total.

In comparison, Russia has slightly fewer active troops but a larger reserve component, mainly comprising ex-conscripts, while China has a soldier population of over 7 billion. Nevertheless, the US beats these two countries in military spending, meaning the country can equip and sustain its soldiers for a longer period in times of war.

In fact, US military spending has risen from $598.5 billion in 2015 to $610 billion in 2017. In comparison, Russia's much smaller military budget that dropped due to inflationary causes from the 2014 $69.3 billion budget to $52 billion in 2015 has risen again in 2017 but only to the tune of $66.3 billion. As for China, which comes second to the US in military spending, its corresponding budget was $131 billion in 2014, but over the following two years it rose to reach $146 billion in 2016 and rose again in 2017 to reach $151.43 billion.

On the overall, US military budget exceeds that of China, Russia that rates third globally, Saudi Arabia, India, France, the UK and Japan collectively. Is US military might sufficient assurance it will maintain its global super power status? As it were, there are more serious acts of aggression today than military interference. It only takes some unscrupulous technology savvy individuals, for example, to bring down or corrupt an entire country's communication system, and considering how central communication is in running day to day affairs, technology certainly comes top in modern day safety.

At the same time, with modern day advanced technology, even during conventional wars countries can launch their attack or defense without sending troops to the battleground. This fact has been exemplified in recent years by the behavior of North Korea, China, the US and South Korea, which involved long distance missile launches. This in essence means that where a country lacks in military might, if it is highly advanced in technology, it could be just as lethal.

It is worth noting that historically, owing to the need for massive numbers of military personnel and machinery, world super powers have for a long time comprised of the big countries only. During the years of the Cold War, those super powers were America and the USSR, and when the Soviet Union disintegrated, Russia, the biggest state in the union, still remained a global power. However, since many states that fell off the USSR proceeded to form other alliances that did not include Russia, America has always appeared to be the global super power post the Cold War. One reason that made these traditional super powers retain their status was that the smaller nations depended on them to help rebuild their countries after the inevitable destruction caused by wars. These matters are, understandably, intertwined with social issues, and so the super powers ended up influencing matters of economy and politics across the globe.

That scenario contrasts significantly with present day dynamics. Now tiny countries that are highly advanced in technology feel confident they can stand on their own economically even when they do not have large military forces to earn them global respect, and so they do not need to be subservient to any power. Estonia, for example, a country with a tiny population of 1.5 million people that was once part of the Soviet Union has a digitally advanced populace, and as Taavi Kotka, once a software company CEO in Estonia explains, the level of digitization Estonia has reached enhances the country's security.

### The Role of Technology on War Outcomes

One aspect of technology is the numerous avenues it provides for transmission of information. Their wide variety and their effectiveness influences what actions are taken in the field and how this is done. In fact, technology today is a necessity as far as ensuring a good flow of information within command chains and control systems. A country whose population, including the military, is well equipped technologically can easily wage information warfare against other countries.

For one it is easy to gather intelligence far and wide and communicate it fast through modern technology, and such efficiency can influence a country's preparedness for potential aggression of all kinds. For a country with intention to put another on its defensive without mobilizing war tanks, it can do this through propaganda particularly since with modern technology word spreads extremely fast. On the other hand, a country that has an advanced communication network can quickly and easily launch a damage control campaign if another country were to launch propaganda against it.

With advanced technology, even a small country can put the command structure of a big military force in disarray by strategically or remotely interfering with its command and control systems. Certainly if there are difficulties in issuing instructions to the forces on the ground, and even in the delivery of feedback from the field to the command centre, it would be very difficult, if not impossible, to coordinate and control the forces, a situation that is a sure recipe for disaster for the affected country.

All in all, information warfare is real in this era, and it can do damage to a country's political and economic status faster than military war, especially because technology connects many facets of the society. For instance, whatever word goes out into the public arena, courtesy of communication technology, has an impact on the financial and stock markets, and depending on the nature of the information, the value of a country's currency and its stocks could either soar or plummet with speed.

Since, as has already been noted, world economies are now interlinked to form a global economy, malicious misinformation can quickly cripple a country's economy if the situation is not contained in good time. Needless to say, a crumbling economy can easily lead to destabilization of a country politically, a fact that has been witnessed in the past when economic sanctions against a country have led to civil unrest and subsequently the overthrow of the regime.

With the world being several years into advanced technology, people now generally understand how useful, and at the same time, disastrous, information can be, depending on who has access to it and how they use it. It is not surprising that countries comparatively smaller than the US, Russia and China are now in the forefront in information technology. Such countries include Iceland, South Korea,

Switzerland, Denmark, UK, Netherlands, Norway and Luxembourg. Finland, Singapore, Sweden and Japan are also doing well in ICT (information communication technology). The reality is that such countries have leverage over countries with large military forces but whose ICT level is still low.

As Captain Paulo Fernando Viegas Nunes, a military engineer, explains, it can be disastrous for the basic decision cycle to be interrupted in times of war, yet armies are today exposed to that risk. The decision cycle within the military, he notes, entails observation, orientation, decision making and action, which he abbreviates as OODA.

If communication is broken at the onset, it would not be possible to make any observation, whether your troops are safe or not, well supplied or not and so on. Without observation, obviously, there is lack of information, and in this case it would be impossible to orientate the attention of the people in charge as the situation requires. Consequently, no informed decision can be made, and certainly appropriate action cannot be taken. In short, today's emerging global super power will, inevitably, be one with advanced technology among other qualities.

### *Economic Might Is A Big Superpower Determinant*

A country with a starving population and failing infrastructure cannot help but submit to the whims of other countries providing aid. With this in mind, it is obvious a country's economic status must play a role in determining its position on the global arena. Although the US has more or less been the undisputed global superpower since the Berlin Wall fell back in 1989, tides are now changing due to China's global economic impact. Different people now hold different views as to which economy is more dominant between the US and China, and it may just be a matter of time before there is a clear distinction between the two.

As at 2017, the two giant economies constituted 39% of the world's GDP and 23% of the world's population, but a survey done by Pew Research Center, a non-partisan group based in Washington DC, people from across the world are torn almost by half in their opinion as to which of the two countries have more economic might, with the US having a slight lead with a 42% vote over China that had 32%. Incidentally, many of US European allies, including France, Germany and the UK consider China the more powerful economy.

Together with Australia, Sweden, Spain and Canada, these countries consider China the new global economic superpower.

### *A Country with Currency Leverage Has Immense Power*

As has been pointed out already, it is easy for countries to submit to their benefactors when their economies are in danger of collapsing, as is the case with North Korea's new appeal to the US. It is likely North Korea changed its tune from one of threats of aggression to one of willingness to cooperate with the US on advice from its historic benefactor, China. Although North Korea President, Kim Jong Un, makes it appear as if his new behavior has nothing to do with the dire economic situation in his country, the reality is that he would like the US to encourage China to relax or lift the economic sanctions China has imposed on North Korea for months, of course, on US instigation.

The reason China is likely to come out the winner is that for all the years the US has threatened North Korea with dire consequences, the regime has never caved in to promise a stoppage to its provocative actions – expansion of its nuclear weapon program as well as testing long-range missiles. Yet now that China has imposed economic sanctions on

North Korea, the small country with notoriety has extended a hand of friendship to the US and pledged to be friendly to its age old nemesis, South Korea. North Korea's behavior is, therefore, a roundabout way of submitting to China. In short, although North Korea's promise of good behavior has been directed at the US, it is only a way of nursing US ego and to encourage the administration to ease the pressure the US has put on China to maintain economic sanctions on North Korea.

This becomes very clear when one takes into consideration the fact that the US has never targeted North Korea as a potential trade partner, because US' largely free market economy and North Korea's government controlled economy are simply not compatible. North Korea's apparent change of attitude towards the US is, therefore, more manipulative than a genuine change of heart, and Kim Jong Un is not the only leader who is in dire need of an image change. President Trump could do with an image boost as well, after having upset several countries with his antagonistic stances on a range of issues of global and social concerns.

With the biting economic sanctions, North Korea's economy is crumbling, and its currency, the "North Korean won", has nosedived in value. Many North Koreans are even said to carry around their money in US dollars or the Chinese Yuan. China has an even upper hand when it comes to controlling the behavior of North Korea, which is its free supply of crude oil to the country. China has not cut off supply to North Korea yet it could, and North Korea would not want that to happen. So, it has to heed China's wish.

It also means the US is at the mercy of China when it comes to having the economic noose tightened around North Korea's neck, because there is nothing of economic value that the US can withhold from North Korea. North Korea's economy, like everything else in the country, is still government controlled, and so the US has not found a way of penetrating the market the way it has in South Korea. North Koreans too do not rely on anything from the US. This status means the US has nothing of economic value to withhold from North Korea as a punitive measure, and therefore it can only rely on China to do so.

If Trump can come across as the leader who tamed the rogue North Korea, the credit can be a real image boost during his presidency, and it would serve as great legacy for him after his term ends. However, it is not easy to tell whether North Korea will hold its side of the bargain, whose details are not clear since no outright promises were formerly made public after the meeting between the leaders of the two countries. The only thing that is indisputable for now is that China has played a big role in getting the two archrivals, the US and North Korea, to hold a historic cordial talk. This announces to the world that China has become very influential both regionally and globally; a great recipe for world superpower status.

## *Ingredients for the Ultimate Superpower*

Clearly, the country most likely to become the world's strongest superpower is the one with a combination of the most important factors required in the modern age: a robust economy and advanced technology. In the case of China, the ICT market sector is locally very dynamic, and it has greatly contributed to China's economic success. In fact, China happens to be the second largest market for ICT products, going by the records of 2017. It is estimated that by 2020, China's ICT market will have hit the $844 billion dollar mark. These estimates that have been provided by a renowned ICT firm, IDC, also indicate that when China's ICT imports were $528 billion, the country's ICT exports were $781 billion. The report highlighted China's continued improvement of its ICT hardware and software as well as services as having helped to enhance the country's global competitiveness in this sector.

In comparison, consumption in the US ICT market is set to hit $351 billion sometime in 2018, this being a 3.9% growth from 2017. In addition, the US relies heavily on imports from China for ICT parts, especially for Smartphones, and with the persistent strain in trade relations between the US and China that began with the Trump administration, prices of key ICT components appear to have hiked. This development is expected to slow down the growth of the sector, and in the meantime China continues to export similar products to Africa, Europe and other parts of the world.

What is likely to hurt the US economy following the hike in tariffs on some Chinese vehicles that was met with retaliatory action by China, is that US' threat to impose higher tariffs on electronics and ICT products from China is bound to hurt the American consumer even more, because the manufacturers who use those imports are bound to raise the prices of the final product. If, on the other hand, the US government raises tariffs on Smartphones, TVs and computers as it is said to be contemplating, the market will dampen. As it were, consumers in the US are being very careful with their discretionary spending.

The issue of which country is the best suited to be accorded the global superpower status is, understandably, controversial, and that is because different people are bound to look at the status from different perspectives. For instance, in the survey that showed Australia, UK and a number of European countries choosing China for qualification as a global superpower, many countries of Africa and Latin America gave their vote to the US. Certainly, countries from either side of the divide had their solid reasons for giving a nod to either China or the US.


## Conclusion

In this book I have provided well researched information and in some cases shown different perspectives to issues. Whether you concur with me or not is not my motive. What is important is that you evaluate each situation with a critical mind, because even for analysts, there are often factors that influence their stance, sometimes at a sub-conscious level. When it comes to the US administration's position on both domestic and global affairs, for instance, one must remember there are two dominant political sides that are likely to hold strong divergent views, and outsiders tend to align themselves with either side.

At the same time, things are changing very fast for different countries due to globalization, and some of the predictions made today might turn out different due to changing markets and political dynamics. Nevertheless, whichever country emerges as the next global superpower, it cannot sit on its laurels because others are continually striving to do better economically. In any case, with advanced technology spreading like wildfire even to countries that were obscure a couple of decades ago, global alliances formed might just bar a single country from emerging as an outright superpower.

In conclusion my advice would be not to take the word of the media at face value. Instead, do your own research and due diligence, and then formulate your own informed opinion. It is imperative that you be sharp in what you hold as true or reject as false, as there is only one truth and that is what prevails at the end of the day.

www.ingramcontent.com/pod-product-compliance
Lightning Source LLC
Chambersburg PA
CBHW070132260726
48658CB00001B/383